GW00692409

# Whom Do I Trust?
# A Practical Guide

## By Shaman Elder Maggie Wahls

From the Modern Spirituality Series

Marvelous Spirit Press

Learn more about the author and what she teaches at
www.ShamanElder.com

eISBN: 978-1-61599-133-4
ISBN-13: 978-1-61599-134-1 (paperback)

Published by
Marvelous Spirit Press, an imprint of
Loving Healing Press
5145 Pontiac Trail
Ann Arbor, MI 48105

Fax 734-663-6861
Tollfree (USA/CAN) 888-761-6268
London, England 44-20-331-81304

www.MarvelousSpirit.com
info@LovingHealing.com

# Contents

# Contents

# What is Trust?

Whom can you trust? You have been lied to, cheated and betrayed many times in your life. We all have. It seems that you cannot trust anyone these days, or at least that is what we have been taught and life experience has confirmed, isn't it?

First, let me introduce myself... my name is Maggie Wahls. My Shaman grandmother began my training at the age of 3, almost 60 years ago now, and from my earliest memories she taught me what trust is and how to be trustworthy. I have been spiritually counseling and teaching traditional Shamanism to people from all walks of life for many decades. I have been given the mission to bring the knowledge of the Traditional Shaman into the modern day world; this is my gift to you.

Trust is something that man in ancient times learned from the Shaman of his tribe. It was the Shaman's example as a member of that tribe or community that showed the people how and why to be trustworthy. It is not something that we learn in our modern day society because Shamanism has been all but lost to modern man. But trust is essential to our relationships with each other and with the Creator. The wisdom in this eBook brings you ancient teachings from my ancestors and your ancestors, passed down through generations for healing everyone's life.

Trust means knowing a certain amount of vulnerability. Trusting means you are not always in control. True vulnerability means trusting and *knowing* that we are all okay on this journey, that we are loved and lovable, and that we are incredible beings who have come here to learn and to grow. Because of this knowledge, you can trust yourself to go through the tests of character that open the way to experiencing your own inner happiness.

But we are taught *not* to be vulnerable, aren't we? We consider vulnerability a weakness, just like asking for help; but can we learn and grow in our vulnerability? Yes, if we understand that vulnerability means trusting that you are okay. We have some very misguided beliefs about trust in this generation.

Let's consider the belief or fear that life can't be trusted and that you will not be okay. Where did we learn that?

- Our parents and society
- Our childhood
- Church

- Negative life experiences

Why would people lead you to accept this belief? Because they were taught to do so.

If you were to teach a child not to trust, what reason would you have to do so? What would you be trying to get from that child?

- Adoration
- Obedience
- Their dependence upon you
- To make sure they stay safe
- All of the above

Do our parents want us to be obedient and depend on them? Yes! So, of course, they teach us the belief or fear that life can't be trusted and that you will not be okay.

But you are an adult now. Do you still need to keep this belief and be dependent and obedient? Why not choose today to believe, trust, and KNOW that we are all okay on this journey, that we are all loved and lovable, and that we are incredible beings who have come here to learn and grow?.

## What is Control?

Let's talk about control because it is also related. Thinking that we can control life leads to a form of spiritual confusion and misconception. Control develops because there *is* fear there: a fear of chaos, or a fear that somehow you aren't capable or adequate in some way and that life will spin out of control, etc. We cannot control life.

Who taught us this fear that leads to our need to control? Again, it was our churches, our parents, and our grandparents who taught us this fearful way of being. Why did they teach us this? So we would be dependent and obedient! They taught us this fear to help control us and make us need them, so we would do what is required by them. And they feared for our safety and thought instilling fear in us would ultimately protect us from doing what might harm us. But as the people we are today, the adults here, do we still need this belief? Aren't we capable now of taking care of ourselves? Do we need to be dependent and live in this man-created fear? No.

What would be a better belief than believing we are not capable, that life will spin out of control?

- Having an incredible trust in our spiritual guides and angels
- Believing that we are okay and that our lives will be okay
- Believing that we are capable of doing anything
- We are spiritual beings having an earthly experience! When we go home to heaven, or whatever you like to call it, are we really hurt in any way by anything that happens here? No. There is nothing here that can hurt the real true eternal you, so you are okay!

There is a need to be committed to self-love, forgiveness, and compassion. As you already recognize, your ability to trust life and to have faith in the future needs to be grown, developed and nurtured. One of the best ways to develop trust is to start expressing gratitude and appreciation. You can express gratitude by practicing thankfulness on a moment-to-moment basis, for all that you have and experience in your life. An attitude of gratitude brings about deep trust and a sense of inner peace toward life. Can you see this?

We have spent years feeling that we are out of control, cannot control, and need to control, when what we really need to see is that we have been given beliefs that made us good children but that do not benefit us now as adults. Let them go!

Pick up a new beneficial belief that you love yourself and forgive yourself since no one here but *you* can judge you.

- Believe in compassion for yourself and others
- Believe in gratitude and appreciation
- Appreciate yourself, for goodness sake!
- And trust that all is in order.

## Letting Go of Control

I love to tell the allegory of this life being like a trip to Disneyland. When you go to Disneyland, is there any *order*? Do you need order for a day in Disneyland? Don't you just run from one ride to the next all day and have fun?

This is what life is meant to be! An adventure! A day in Disneyland! But there is nothing in Disneyland that really harms you. It may look scary like a roller coaster with lots of thrills and spills, but it is not harming the real you.

When you think of yourself as a spiritual being having an earthly existence, you realize that you are so much more than your body! You are so much more than just your feelings or your mind! Do you have any idea how big your spiritual self is? How precious? How important? What you are physically on this earth is only 5% of the total you! Yet this is the only part that we pay attention to. This is the part that is so concerned about the job or the house or keeping up with the Joneses. The Joneses have no idea of All That Is!

When we look at the Dalai Lama, is he concerned about what kind of car he drives? Does he feel his life will spin out of control any minute? He knows that we are all OK!

When you go to Disneyland, do you control the rides? No! You have to trust someone else, don't you? A stranger no less! You seem to have no problem with that. So why do you have a problem giving up control in *this* Disneyland? What is there to control? Why not trust! This life is to be experienced and lived and enjoyed just like Disneyland. You will go home safe and sound, I promise!

Why are we taught to *make something* of our lives? So we can get a good job and have a two-story house like the Joneses? We are here to give of what we already possess. That is our mission but no one taught us this fact.

## Collaborating with the Creator

You are not alone here. The Creator is here with you at all times watching over you, protecting you, listening to you and willing to guide you completely if you will let the Creator guide you.

What do we know about the other 95% of us or the rest of creation? *Not much.* But what does the Creator know? Everything! The Creator created it! So should we be like blind kids groping around in a candy shop or should we listen to the Creator who can tell us what is coming and what is best from the Creator's view? I, for one, would not want to be without the Creator's guidance, even for one millisecond!

What does it take to be in the Creator's guidance?

- It takes a bit of time and effort. That is all. What a great trade!

- It takes you expressing gratitude and thankfulness that you have this intimate personal two-way communication on a moment-to-moment basis.

- An attitude of gratitude proves that you value your connection with the Creator.

If you value this always-available connection to insight, truth, guidance and protection, then you will listen to the Creator. Of course, it is your choice. The Creator will never violate your freewill choice. Freewill choice is one of the greatest gifts the Creator has given to every created thing. The Creator will not take back any gift you have been given. You have freewill to choose what you wish and to create the life you choose for yourself. And you are accountable for your choices, not the Creator.

## Elements of Trust

There are five elements to trust. Anyone you choose to trust should demonstrate all five of these qualities consistently.

- Reliability
- Consistency
- Truthfulness
- Accountability
- Follow-through

In the remainder of this eBook, we'll be examining each one of these elements in turn.

# 1. Reliability

How trustworthy are you? And whom should you trust? This book is meant not only to teach you about how to choose whom to trust in your life, but also to teach you about being trustworthy. We are not taught either of these growing up, and as a result we make errors in whom we trust and get ourselves into trouble. So I want you to study this from both perspectives: trusting others and being trustworthy yourself.

First, I would like to give you some more information about reliability and consistency, the first facets of trust. A person who does as promised can be considered *reliable*. Reliability is an admirable characteristic. People don't like to deal with those who are unreliable. They'd rather give their business and rewards to the person they can count on. Also, the reliable person feels good knowing that he or she is trusted.

Questions you may have are:

- What does it mean to be reliable?
- What is being unreliable?
- How does reliability pay off?

If you promise to do something, you are assumed to be good for your word. Sometimes that promise is implied or presumed. Some people will renege on their word or responsibility for any number of possible reasons.

For example, a person may lie to get out of an uncomfortable or awkward situation and may never have intended to do what was promised. Suppose someone asked you to come over to help with some task, which you did not really care to do. It may be easier to say you will, but then never show up. The other person would likely think you unreliable, especially if this situation happened more than once. Another example is if you agreed to meet someone, but some friends come over and want to take you out. So you never show up to meet your friend because the other activity was more important to you. Being considerate and calling to excuse yourself might feel awkward, so you don't bother.

Suppose a person at work is often late on completing assignments, either because the assignments are too difficult or he gets sidetracked with more interesting activities. His boss and fellow workers consider him unreliable.

Of course, you cannot count on a person who is known to be unreliable and does not follow-through on what he or she has promised to do. A person may promise to pick you up at the airport, but then not show up because "he forgot." Or a person may come to a meeting late because she got involved in some other activity and "lost track of time."

What happens with unreliable people is that they renege on their promises. They are unreliable because of the way they set their priorities. Their promise to *you* is not as important to them as something else. I bet we have all encountered people like this.

Some people actually lack the skills to complete jobs. Some lie and have no intention of doing the job. Some have good intentions but are so forgetful or caught up in their own interests that they either forget or don't bother to do what they promised. Often, what they are really saying is that you aren't as important to them . People who are unreliable at work are saying that the job is not as important to them as some other activity.

A reliable person is one who has a track record of doing what he or she has promised to do. If a person continually completes the tasks she promised to do, she is then considered reliable. If a person says he will show up at 10:30 AM, and he is known to be reliable, you can count on him to be on time. Being considered reliable means that you are conscientious and keep your promises. A reliable person does not make excuses.

Certainly you would want to associate with a person you can count on. Supervisors want to keep employees who are reliable and who they can count on to come to work on time and to complete assigned tasks. Such a person is trusted to do as promised.

The benefit of being reliable is that people trust you and feel they can count on you. A reliable person will get and keep friends much easier than someone who is careless in personal relationships and can't be counted on to keep his or her word. A reliable worker will be trusted to do the job as promised and can reap the rewards in raises and promotions. A business that has a reputation of being reliable or making reliable products will get repeat and new business, as well as reducing costs of rework or repair.

On the negative side, being considered reliable can put you into situations where others can soon take you for granted and not appreciate your reliability. It is a trait of human nature that if something or someone is very predictable, then those actions are not appreciated.

Although it is possible to be taken advantage of by being reliable and predictable, in the long run reliability is the best way. Being reliable is an admirable trait. We all dislike dealing with people who are unreliable, so being reliable is a character trait for which we should strive. People thank you for it. You get a good reputation. You also feel good about yourself when you do as promised. It is a good feeling to be a man or woman "Of your word".

Again, a reliable person has a track record of keeping his or her promises. An unreliable person shows he or she doesn't really care about others. You can't count on such a person. The benefits of being reliable include promotions at work, better personal relationships, and increased self-esteem.

Isn't it interesting that being reliable leads to a better sense of self-esteem? That you can feel better about yourself by learning to be reliable for others? As you give, so you get for yourself! And isn't it interesting that when something is predictable, we do not value it so much? Think about that!

So yes, reliability is certainly part of impeccability. Doing the very best you can do at all times. It is also speaking your truth, isn't it? And it is also about forming an intention and keeping that intention. Reliability is also a shamanic trait.

# 2. Consistency

The second part of reliability is *consistency*, which means that we are stepping up to be reliable all the time, not just sometimes or to certain people or promises. We all know what it means to be consistent. And consistency is part of being trustworthy. Do you see how being reliable and consistent is good for you personally?

Here is a little mini quiz. Just pick the answer that best describes your reaction. Don't over- think it!

1. If you promise to help a friend move on Saturday, but then you start watching a good TV show, what should you do?
    a) He probably has other helpers, so you finish watching the show
    b) Call him and say your grandma died
    c) Keep your word and show up as promised

2. If a friend is always late, would you ask him to take you to the airport?
    a) Yes, but make him promise to be on time
    b) Probably not, because you can't count on him
    c) Yes, but don't be home, so you can teach him a lesson

3. Would you be considered reliable if you are usually on time, except when your car doesn't start?
    a) You are as reliable as your car
    b) An unreliable car is a good excuse for being late
    c) Yes, because you had good intentions

I have asked you to look at yourself as someone people can rely on and also identify who you can trust. I have explained what reliability is in its most fundamental form so that you can understand it fully. I don't want any confusion here! Here is another definition of reliability:

"Systemic reliability is the ability of a system to perform and maintain its functions in routine circumstances, as well as hostile or unexpected circumstances. In natural language it may also denote persons who act efficiently in proper moments/circumstances."

Bill Smith, *Six Sigma*

So it means being reliable even when things get mucked up! An inherent quality of reliability is honesty. If you say you will be there at two, you are there at two, right? And you are consistent.

I am afraid that reliability is no longer being taught to our young people. They are taught that it is fashionable to be late or even worse that other people's time is not important. They cannot trust each other because they have thrown reliability out the window with the bathwater, as my Mom would say!

## Self-Esteem and Self-Respect

Being reliable is a good way to increase your own self-respect. Certainly the advertising media has taught us that there is no truth in advertising. If the advertising media is not truthful, then it is not trustworthy. There is a difference between respect and trust. You can certainly respect someone, but not trust him or her.

I have never had the problem of being so dependable that I was taken for granted. I have more often seen people amazed that I do show up on time every time. I have more often seen people awed by my doing what I say I will do. They just don't encounter this in their own lives, or hardly ever.

I bet you rarely see it in others as well. So what an honor it is to show people what trust is and what being reliable means by being consistently reliable yourself! That is why others need to see it in us as teachers. What a great example you can be. What a great thing to teach by example! And you also develop your own self-esteem at the same time. You feel good about yourself because you are being reliable!

I don't think it takes strength to walk in truth. Rather, I think it takes strength to look in the mirror and see what you are really doing. I think walking in truth is being your authentic self.

Nothing given by Creator is hard or difficult. Man alone makes things hard. Reliability is a virtue, a positive character trait. It should be part of your authenticity. It makes you authentic to be reliable.

Being reliable or not is a freewill choice you make. A short parable may help explain this. There once was a woman who was very trustworthy. She assumed that everyone was trustworthy. She wanted everyone to be trustworthy. And she could not see why people were not reaching for trustworthiness in their own lives. She wanted to teach trustworthiness so she practiced it and practiced it and showed it to everyone around her.

But they rejected what she was teaching and she got upset and frustrated. She knew that trust was valuable and gave her a good sense of self-esteem and she wanted this for everyone. But by trying to make everyone trustworthy, what was she doing? She was violating other people's freewill choice, wasn't she? An even bigger mistake! So she had to understand that it is each person's freewill choice to be trustworthy or not and to let them choose for themselves. She could continue to be an example for those who wished to learn trustworthiness but she should not try to make other people trustworthy against their free will choice.

> "It is what you *do* that defines you!"
> —Traditional Shamanic Truth

If you are trustworthy, reliable, consistent, accountable, truthful, and you practice follow-through, then that is what defines you. That is your character, your authentic self. That is who you are.

Speaking your truth is a choice you make. It builds self-esteem and makes you trustworthy. Speaking your truth is also a component of compassion.

I find people are attracted to me because I speak my truth. In fact, I don't feel any isolation because of it. People regard my speaking my truth as a breath of fresh air in a lying world! People are attracted to other people who speak their truth with compassion.

The only approval that counts is your own approval of yourself. People seek approval because they are not sure that their own beliefs are true beliefs. They also seek approval because they have beliefs that do not benefit them and they want confirmation from others to continue believing in those non-benefiting beliefs. They look for others to tell them to continue believing in those non-benefiting beliefs or others who also believe those non-benefiting beliefs. They look for outside confirmation. The wife beater goes down to the bar to hang around with other wife beaters for confirmation that what he is doing is okay.

That is why we talk about beliefs in the course I teach at www.ShamanElder.com. In my course, you get to chose your own benefiting beliefs so that you can speak your truth. If you don't know what you believe, what truth can you speak?

Do you have to believe what other people believe?

- Who knows you better than you?

- We are all unique.

- No one out there knows what you believe better than you do!

So when you know what you truly believe and you work to make all your beliefs benefit you today, then you will really have some truth to speak.

And if you find out that one of your beliefs no longer benefits you, choose to change it. It is a very easy choice to make.

We speak the truth as we know it in this moment, but we can stay open to changing our beliefs if at any time they do not benefit us.

# 3. Truthfulness

I wanted to talk about the next point in trust, which is truthfulness. But before we begin I want to remind you that we are learning what trust is not so much to make you work on being trustworthy, that is your choice, but more to point out to you ways to know whom you can trust.

When we trust the wrong people we get hurt, don't we? I think it is important to trust the right people. Not everybody is trustworthy. If we assume that, we do get hurt.

It is OK for people to be whoever they are, but I want to know what trust is so I can choose carefully.

## Judgment and a Free Mind

Wow! What does having a free mind and no judgment have to do with truth? Truth is found in perception and unless we perceive clearly, we can't tell what is true. And when we judge, we are putting our own belief system on someone else's head, aren't we? Your truth is not necessarily for everyone, is it?

The following parable will illustrate this point. A group of blind monks were taken to see an elephant for the first time. One by one, each blind monk went up to the elephant. The first one touched its back and exclaimed, "Oh, it is a wall!" The second blind monk touched its trunk and said, "It's a strong pillar!" The third blind monk touched its tail and exclaimed, "It's a rope!" Each monk assumed that the part he touched was the whole thing. Their knowledge of the elephant remained defective, a partial understanding, and imperfect. This is true whenever we gather only a little information about anything before making a judgment. To really know something is to experience it fully.

> "Truthfulness is the firmest road leading to God, and the truthful are fortunate travelers upon it. Truthfulness is the spirit and essence of action and the true standard of straightforwardness in thought; the spirit and essence of action."
>
> *Key Concepts In The Practice Of Sufism: Emerald Hills of the Heart, Vol. 1* By M. Fethullah Gulen

It is pretty hard to move forward in action if you are not truthful, isn't it! And if someone can speak their truth, they pretty much have their heads screwed on straight, don't they!

" A loyal, truthful one changes states at least forty times a day (in order to preserve personal integrity), while a hypocrite remains the same for forty years without feeling any trouble or unease (over his or her deviation)."

Al-Qushayri, *Al-Risala* (p. 211)

"Truthfulness elevates ordinary people to extraordinary heights, and is a key that opens the door to realms and realities beyond visible existence. One borne aloft by truthfulness cannot be detained from journeying upward, and doors are not closed in the face of one who uses this key."

*Key Concepts In The Practice Of Sufism: Emerald Hills of the Heart, Vol. 1* By M. Fethullah Gulen

The Shaman knows this and uses this key of truthfulness always.

What is truthfulness?

- Feelings, thoughts, words and actions that do not contradict each other.

Why is it important to be truthful?

- To gain trust, mostly for ourselves; no self deception; free to be you and me, but let's do it honestly!

If we can't trust ourselves, others will not trust us either. This is true!

Why do people lie?

- Because they believe their truth will not be accepted by others.
- Fear of what people will think.
- Fear of change.
- To protect themselves when they do wrong.

What else might someone be afraid of and thus lie?

- non-acceptance
- fear of confrontation
- fear of getting caught in a lie that perpetuates a bigger lie.

Whose acceptance do you need so badly that you are willing to lie for it?

Is it necessary to have people hold sway over you to the point of lying to gain acceptance? No one has ultimate authority over individual free will choice. Parents love you more for speaking your truth than for lying to gain their acceptance. And it seems to me that if you must lie to your employer to keep your job, maybe it's not the job for you.. If you must lie through thought, word or action to be accepted by a religious community, maybe then you should reconsider belonging to that community.

We are indeed taught to lie! And yes, people lie because it is easier than telling the truth, for sure! But is it being true to you? I want you to be authentic to you, within or without the conventions of the age. And you can!

What problems do you encounter when you are not truthful?
- You need to keep track of whom you lied to and what you said.
- It limits your relationship with the person you lied to.
- It's hard to have meaningful relationships.
- It puts a lump in the chest...makes you doubt yourself.
- It lowers self-esteem.
- You are just not being authentic to you, either.
- It blocks the path to the future.
- The energy shuts down.

And why would we want to lower our self-esteem to be accepted by others? It's a big mistake. I am back to what authority is. Is it worthwhile to lie just to be accepted? The only authority I want to be accepted by is the Creator and I don't have to lie to get that. Outside of that, I will not lie to myself- the other authority figure in my life.

Why do we lie just to be accepted? People think it will boost their ego.

Why do we fear not being accepted by outside authority figures or groups or religious groups?

Conformity is impossible because we are each unique.

Why do we want to be just like everyone else? Everyone else out there is not surviving any better than we are! There is no safety in numbers here.

How do you feel when people have been untruthful with you?

- Angry, actually
- Betrayed.
- Sad
- Hurt
- Resentful

And how do you feel when you have been untruthful with yourself?

- Diminished
- Sad
- Ashamed
- Depressed

You actually feel the same as if someone lied to you, don't you? So is it one of those, "Do as I say not as I do" things?

Why is it not OK for someone to lie to you but it is OK for you to lie to someone else? It's not Ok. We are back to self-esteem and authenticity, aren't we!

What is a half-truth?

- withholding part of the information
- making a lie sound like it is not a lie, but it still is
- it is a lie that has a thin line of reality

How about saying something nice when you don't mean it? Or not telling the truth because it might offend someone? This is back to lying to gain acceptance.

Telling the truth should be done with compassion and without harming others with your words.

"A mind that is subject to desire and anger will not give rise to words that bespeak affection and cause well-being. Truthful words that create good are the product of a mind free from desire and anger."

—Sri Sri Sri Chandrasekharendra Saraswathi MahaSwamiji

So here we see how to tell the truth.

There should be no ulterior motives in your truth.

Have you noticed how your emotions color your truth. Sarcasm, for example, completely undermines the truth of a statement. How you speak your truth is important too. A snide remark, talking behind someone's back and getting people to do what you want by your words are all half truths. These are technically lies. Using your truth to make people do something that you want them to do is a lie. For example, a little child who is afraid to sleep in his dark bedroom is told there is a boogey man under the bed and he stays in his bed, too afraid to get up. Is this good?

When you are happy with what you have, whatever that is, you don't need to manipulate. And when you are happy living in each day fully; you don't need an agenda.

The practice of truthfulness has two things that we should keep in mind: first, it is a "practice." One has to practice it consistently; it is a continuing effort that one strives to practice every day. Secondly, in the Indian philosophy of Yoga, truth also means the concept that the "Self"—the soul—is One, all-pervading, everlasting, ever pure, ever free. The "Self" in me is the same one as the "Self" in you. Knowing this, that all beings are essentially one, that everything is interconnected, it then becomes easier for us to see where the practice of truthfulness and non-hurting comes from. The meaning of the word "truth" is not just what we normally associate with it—not just saying straight-out lies.

If you practice truthfulness for some time, you will see the effects of this practice. You will notice how this becomes the 'practice of non-hurting' any other sentient beings (not just people). And this 'non-hurting' again is operative on the three levels of thought, speech, and actions. It is quite amazing.

"You must accept yourself as you are, instead of as you would like to be, which means giving up self-deception and wishful thinking. As long as you regard yourself or any part of your experience as "the dream come true," then you are involved in self-deception. If we really want to learn and see the experience of truth, we have to be where we are."
— Chogyam Trungpa, *Cutting Through Spiritual Materialism*

## Self-Deception

Self-deception! How many people live in self-deception? Living in the past or living in the future is self-deception. It seems to me the only way to not be deceiving yourself, is to live in the now. We could never know the whole or absolute truth about anything but we can be truthful in telling what we do know and understand. The standard test for right conduct including truthfulness is harmlessness.

Being true in your endeavors will help you gain others' trust and enhance your success. Whenever there is a task, you must put your heart into it.

Is truthfulness a responsibility? A responsibility to whom?

- To Creator and ourselves and our guides.
- To ourselves first.
- To all of us.

So what I am saying is that if you consider yourself responsible then you are truthful. Do you hold others to a similar, or higher, standard of honesty than you practice? And why do we hold others to a higher standard of honesty than we hold ourselves? Why is it ok for us to lie but not for the President to lie?

Do you know that it is only you who judges you? Why is it so hard to be honest with yourself, if you are the judge and jury anyway? You have forgiven tons of people in your lifetime; can you not forgive yourself a bit? Who makes this life so hard anyway? To be honest, I bet you can see many qualities and gifts and talents that you have. I bet you can see that you are a pretty good person! It doesn't matter what others think. It matters what you honestly think of yourself. It doesn't matter if you are accepted by others, if you can accept yourself fully. Kind of linked together, aren't they? So why not look at yourself honestly and see all the wonderful bits and parts of you! Sure we are human; sure we make mistakes and have foibles; that makes the colors on the quilt of humanity. How boring if we were all perfect! Accept your foibles as part of your human nature and just do your impeccable best. Creator doesn't create anything flawed. You are exactly as Creator intended you! He wanted you to be human with foibles! So, accept your foibles; know what they are and do your best to keep them under control. I have not met anyone without foibles.

Foibles are flaws, imperfections, quirky habits, etc. Creator does not look upon you and see only your flaws. Creator sees your entire self and loves you very much just as you are. Why not start to love yourself in the same way? And love others no matter what their foibles are, too! This will allow you to be honest with yourself and with others. But it is a practice. Take baby steps. It is the easy way!

# 4. Accountability

Anyone remember the five parts of trust? Let's review them again:

- Reliability
- Consistency
- Truthfulness
- Accountability
- Follow-through

> "It is not only what we do, but also what we do not do, for which we are accountable."
>
> —Moliere

In essence, self-accountability is the cornerstone of a moral and responsible way of living. It is about who we are as people on our own paths of life as well as what we do when no one is watching. When we have a well-developed sense of self-accountability, we are honest with ourselves, answerable and fully responsible for what we say and do at all times. We need to have the ability to look beyond the immediate moment to consider all the consequences and know if we are willing to accept them. If a person is not known to live this way, then maybe they should not deserve your trust.

Accountability is an age-old truth that says you are answerable for both your actions and inactions. If something happens or something goes wrong, it's you who must take responsibility. There's a small difference between "It's not finished" and "I haven't finished it." The willingness to be accountable for what you do and what you fail or refuse to do is a benchmark of trustworthiness.

Unaccountable people are good at making excuses, blaming others, putting things off, doing only the minimum, acting confused and pretending to be helpless. They say they are helpless or not aware while hiding behind walls of their own making, e.g. computers, paperwork, and other people. They say things like," I didn't know"."I wasn't there". "I don't have time". "It's not my job". "That's just the way I am". "Nobody told me". Unaccountable people are quick to complain or blame others and slow to act. Perhaps you can think of examples of this. And perhaps you can see that this unaccountability is a benchmark of untrustworthiness.

These are examples of using diversionary tactics: an action, excuse, or belief a person hides behind that justifies his or her behavior and performance. Diversionary tactics provide a person with the "out" so they do not have to be accountable for their performance, responsibilities, goals or the situations they put themselves in. How many times have you been frustrated by these flimsy excuses for not doing or saying what needed to be done or said?

How accountable are you? Does it depend on the situation or are you always ready to accept responsibility for your decisions and behaviors? On a scale of 1-10, with 1 representing "Never" and 10 representing "Always," rank yourself on each of these characteristics of accountability. They apply equally well to professional and personal situations.

1.   If I don't understand something, I seek out information.
2.   I own my own problems and circumstances.
3.   When I make a mistake, I admit it.
4.   I am proactive, often taking the initiative.
5.   I ask for the things I need to do my job.
6.   I analyze my activities and ask, "How is this contributing to organizational objectives?" I analyze my activities and ask, "What more can I do?"
7.   I stand and deliver when it's time to report on my actions.
8.   I welcome feedback.
9.   I model accountability for the people I work with and supervise.
10.  I readily confront unaccountable behavior in others.

Obviously, the higher the score, the better you did. Take a second look at items on which you ranked yourself at the low end of the scale. What can you do to become more accountable in those areas?

Being accountable is one of the fastest ways to earn respect, trust, and promotions. More importantly, it puts you in control of your life. Responding accountably to life's challenges gives you the power to change things. That's the biggest benefit of all.

Life is full of choices. Being responsible means being in charge of our choices and, thus, our lives. It means being accountable for what we do and who we are. It also means recognizing that our actions matter and we are morally on the hook for the consequences. We are in control of our own lives.

This is very important. An accountable person is not a victim and doesn't shift blame or claim credit for the work of others. He considers the likely consequences of his behavior and associations. He leads by example. Are you a victim? Is the person you are deciding to put your trust in showing himself or herself as a victim?

Do you know what you are accountable for? Make a list of those things you have trusted yourself to do or someone else is trusting you to do. What do you want to be accountable for this week?

I want to speak more personally about diversionary tactics that sabotage accountability for a minute here. Again, please don't take these solely as personal criticisms or get down on yourself about it but remember that we are looking at this to determine whom we can trust as well. I want to bring accountability down home to where we live here so you can understand it.

You know that there are activities or tasks that you may be more comfortable doing (such as cleaning your office, doing paperwork, responding to e-mails, helping other people), but which don't significantly move you forward. Instead, they keep you stuck in maintenance mode, allowing you to do just enough to stay afloat. Then, you may have conversations with yourself that sound like, "That's okay, I was busy today. I'll do that tomorrow." Or, "I just wasn't able to find the time to get to that thing I said I would do today." And wouldn't you know it, something else always seems to come up!

This busy work will disguise the truth, creating the illusion that you're working hard, simply because you feel busy. These diversionary tactics enable you to do everything else but the activities that would allow you to progress in your life. This busywork becomes never-ending, an exercise in futility. Consider that these things you have decided or agreed to do, but that you may be avoiding, must become as habitual as waking up in the morning, taking a shower, brushing your teeth, and breathing. These are the activities you do, (hopefully) without a second thought.

## Diversionary Tactics to Avoid

Let's take a look at some psychological diversionary tactics most people use.

**Fear of failure or success:** "I'm afraid of failure, yet I won't take the steps to ensure my success at anything. Therefore, if I sit back and do nothing, then I can never fail at anything!" (Ever know anyone like this?)

**Perfectionism:** "Either I become the perfect concert pianist or I don't practice at all. There's no middle ground here. Therefore, I can't practice piano just yet because my practice isn't perfect! Once I create the perfect system, then I will begin to practice." (And when will that be?)

**Doing Everything Yourself:** "I can't allow others to do these tasks that they may be able to do because they will never do it as good as I can. Therefore, it's just easier if I do it myself. That's why I never have enough time to walk my path." (Great, now you can become an expert in busywork or the activities that aren't the best use of your time or skills, rather than the activities that are going to help you grow and progress in your own life.)

**Been There, Done That:** "The last time I studied yoga, it was a waste of my time. Therefore, I know that studying yoga won't work for me. (Did you ever consider that it was more about your approach to yoga that wasn't effective? If you change your approach, you change your results, so be careful about learning the wrong lesson.)

**Too Busy to Plan:** "I'm so busy that I don't have the time to create my routine!" (You allow your schedule to hold you accountable for doing what you need to do to create the results and the lifestyle you want. Your routine is where your day starts and where it ends. After all, life works a whole lot easier when you do what you say you are going to do.)

**Distraction:** Do you become easily diverted or distracted by situations, new tasks or people rather than focus on your goals and initial objective? If so, you probably have a long list of tasks that never gets completed, because you feel that you're always being pulled in a different direction. (And who's responsible for that?) You may also be habituated to overload and love the rush associated with working on overdrive when trying to do it all.

**Victimhood:** Do you allow one bad experience to snowball and affect the rest of your day? Rather than moving on and forging ahead, this allows you to go into a negative tailspin and destroy the chance of doing anything else productive for the remainder of your day, or your life.

While you may find that one or two (or more) of these behaviors describe some of your diversionary tactics, this is actually good news! Hey, I never said that you would actually like bringing this truth to the surface. After all, it takes a lot of courage to admit our foibles. However, now that you have a greater understanding and awareness about them, you can do something about it.

When you notice yourself falling into these traps, you can make the choice either to continue in your diversionary tactic or make a better choice that will bring the results you really want. There are so many people in this world who are trying to get you to trust them. So I think that now we have a better understanding of what accountability really means and we can see that when people ask us to trust them who also exhibit these diversionary tactics, we might want to think a little harder about trusting them.

You know, the most interesting part is that you choose what you wish to be accountable for! You are responsible for the choices you make and you are free to make your own choices. You are not accountable for the guy next door. It might help to make a list of what you choose to be accountable for. It might help to make a list of what you wish to accomplish in your life and put a timeline on those things.

Either you are going to run your day, or other people and circumstances are going to run you. Honor the commitments you make to others as well as the commitments you make to yourself.

How can someone be accountable to others if they are not accountable to themselves?

At the end of the day, I take stock of what I have accomplished in that one day. You are not accountable to other people's expectations, only your own expectations. But if you say you will do something for someone, then you chose to be accountable to that person for that thing.

Your own expectations for you should not be difficult. Why make your life so hard?

Aha! Now we know why our lives seem so very hard! We set expectations that are too high for ourselves!

Each day I set expectations for that one day. At the end of the day I see what I have accomplished. If I have a setback, oh well, I start again tomorrow. It is just one day! It has been said that having too many expectations is the way to cause yourself the worst emotional problems.

I receive the Creator's appreciation for being reliable and consistent and accountable and truthful and having to follow-through. I give myself appreciation for a job well done as well.

There is an old saying that goes, "If you are constantly being disappointed, just lower your expectations." I find that is really true. We disappoint ourselves and keep ourselves in a rut of failure by choosing impossible expectations for ourselves. Why not take it easy on ourselves.

So accountability is really a way for you to clean house and accept responsibility for what you choose to be accountable for. You make the list, not anyone else. You decide how hard your life is going to be tomorrow! And when you meet someone using diversionary tactics or playing the victim or setting up so many expectations that it is impossible to fulfill them all, maybe this someone is not able to be trusted. They cannot trust themselves. Should you trust them?

# 5. Follow-through

Now we are going to talk about the last part of trust. Do you remember the five parts of trust?

- Reliability
- Consistency
- Truthfulness
- Accountability
- Follow-through

Having these five traits is probably a good indication that the person can be trusted. It's good to know who to trust and who not to trust.

All five traits would be exhibited consistently because consistency is one of the traits. So what is follow-through? Accountability is different from follow-through. You can fail to follow-through and still be accountable for your failure. What are some other words that mean *follow-through*?

I like to think of my golf swing and how important the follow-through is there. The ball won't go anywhere if I stop swinging where the ball sits, right? How about closing, completion, mop up, closing the deal, making good on your choice or promise or the obligation you took upon yourself. We have to mop up what we say we will do, right? How can you trust someone who says he will do something and then never does? So follow-through on your own choices is really important.

To be trustworthy, a person must follow-through in word and action. To be trustworthy to yourself you also have to mop up what you choose to commit to. What does it cost you when you do not follow-through on your own choices or commitments to yourself or others?

- Self-esteem
- Integrity

No one is meant to be perfect, but we can be impeccable which means to do our very best.

I am a traditional Shaman and I have been spiritually counseling people for over 35 years from all walks of life and teaching traditional Shamanism for ten years now.

Let me share with you what a client I counseled wrote to me about follow-through:

"This really made me think about all the things I've said I would or wanted to do. There's always a low-level feeling of guilt about them, so I made a list of everything I could remember, and that I looked at it carefully to see whether I'd overcommitted. Since I "don't work outside the home" (as the saying goes) I think I have unlimited time so when someone asks me to help with something I say yes. Not just because I don't like saying no—maybe not even because I don't like saying no. For me, it's more a matter of liking to help, to be needed, to be counted on for my skills and knowledge. So I keep taking on new things without considering how it would affect things I've already committed to. But no more! From now on, I'm going to think carefully about the choices I make"

—SH

Notice what her real motivations for her commitments are. What does she state as her real reason for promising more than she can follow-through on?

- To be appreciated, perhaps.
- To be trusted actually, but who can trust her when she cannot follow-through.
- She over-commits.

## Ulterior Motives

She has created a vicious circle here! A lot of people have ulterior motives for committing to things. It is important to know why you commit to something: for praise, for self-esteem, to be "big," to be important, to gain admiration, to be applauded, or to be looked up to, and of course, not being able to say no!

What is the ulterior motive for someone to agree to do something for you? What are they getting out of that favor? Are they giving freely or is this really a barter for something you're not aware of, something you're not expecting, something you would not agree to if you knew this was a barter? This is another trap we fall into when we trust someone who is not trustworthy. Someone says, "Oh sure! I would be happy to do that for you!" And then down the road they are demanding that you repay them in some way, that you give them something in return for what you thought was a gift or a favor. It seems like a betrayal, doesn't it? But in truth it was a barter from the beginning. You just didn't know it.

People who pretend to give freely and are actually bartering are not being truthful, are they! So to protect yourself it is OK to ask straight out, "Is this a gift or a barter." You want to know if it is barter and decide for yourself what you will trade and if it is worth trading for. There is nothing wrong with asking right out whether they are bartering or giving freely. And a trustworthy person will tell you the truth. There is nothing wrong with a barter unless the other party is not aware that it is, in truth, a barter. Then, it is stealing.

Do you know people who always put off the hard tasks? Or who let unpleasant tasks pile up? Or who make more promises than they can keep? There is no follow-through there, is there? Are these the people you feel comfortable trusting? Do you see how follow-through is a part of trust?

Some of the personal consequences of not following through are loss of health, lack of self respect, just giving up, never starting anything because one knows it will not get done. What a shame not to go for it because of one's own failure to follow-through.

So how do we foster follow-through? We foster follow-through with humility, awareness, self-respect, commitment to oneself and integrity. How about having more good intentions in the first place?

A good intention means that you value that intention enough to invest in it and follow-through on it. How about really knowing why you are doing something and not losing sight of the reasons for doing it. Sometimes we forget why we said we would do something, especially when it gets a bit difficult.

But if you know the reasons you chose to do something you will more likely see it through to completion. So here is where awareness comes in: being aware of the thing and its path and what it will take before you ever commit to it.

Many people make a good start but get distracted or just give up, and never get where they wanted to go. Some really never intended to put in the necessary work. Others may just need to adopt the mantra, "Slow and steady wins the race."

If you have lapses, don't waste any energy at all beating yourself up for them. Put them behind you and tell yourself that only one thing matters: not giving up. No matter how badly you may have performed recently, as long as you start again, you have not given up and all is well.

Finally, enjoy yourself! Accomplishing big things is hard work, but it is also exciting and fun. Allow yourself to have a relaxed attitude. Be confident that you are doing what you should, that things are working as they should, and that your results are coming. Make good choices about what you commit your time and effort to.

Life is always changing, and your goals change along the way as well. Since you will always be going somewhere, you need to be able to enjoy the trip. This will keep you from burning out along the way, and perhaps even more importantly, when you succeed, it will make your successes meaningful.

I want to share something from the *Boy Scouts Handbook* that we can all take to heart:

> "Often, we hear people asking someone to 'Step Up' to a challenge that needs to be done. Stepping Up means that you have accepted the responsibility, not of Starting that job, but of Finishing it. Before you stepped up, you were in a comfortable position, no stress, no effort being put out—kind of like just standing here. You could stand here for an hour easily. You aren't getting anywhere, but it's easy. Once you 'Step Up' to a challenge, it is no longer comfortable. Others now expect you to perform. You have work to do and it may be difficult. It's like Stepping Up onto this chair.
>
> (step one foot onto the chair seat, keeping only the toes of the other foot on the floor)
>
> This is a difficult position. It isn't comfortable. I haven't accomplished anything and I can't stay here long. I have to do something. So, I 'Follow-through'—I complete all the work required for the task and I do what I said I would do. (stand with both feet on the chair)
>
> Now, I'm comfortable again. I could stand here forever with no effort.
>
> If I never Step Up to a challenge, then I never grow.
>
> If I Step Up to a challenge, but do not Follow-through, nothing gets done and I let down everyone that counted on me.
>
> When I Step Up and Follow-through, then I succeed, I grow, and others know they can count on me."

When you follow-through, people can count on you; they can trust you.

What a beautiful thing to put in the Boy Scout manual. How important for all of us to understand follow-through and its relationship to trustworthiness.

# Conclusion

I have given you this five part teaching on trust because we don't know who we can trust anymore, because we get hurt trusting the wrong people, because Creator wants you to know who you can trust and who not to. Whether it is choosing a teacher or giving your money to someone, trust is so important.

No one wants to see you getting hurt by not knowing what trust really is. There is easy learning as we have here or there is hard learning like getting burnt. I try to give you easy learning here. So I hope you will remember the five facets of trust and use them as a measuring stick when dealing with people. If you can apply them to your own life, so much the better, but that is not the point of this book.

You need to be aware of who is trustworthy and who is not. If someone is not consistent or accountable, if someone does not follow-through or speak the truth, let the flags go up in your mind from what you have learned in this eBook.

If someone is not reliable, let your ears prick up and the goose bumps rise up on your skin so that you become aware of what is going on. We walk in power and we don't need to create pits to fall into. Awareness and knowledge can be gained in an easy way to avoid falling into pits if you choose to take the wisdom. Creator always prefers to teach us the easy way.

The true, authentic Shaman is completely trustworthy. These five qualities of trustworthiness are the backbone of Traditional Shamanism. If a Shaman is not trustworthy, then that Shaman has no self-esteem and no personal power. And if that Shaman has no personal power then that Shaman has nothing you want! And if my ancestors were not trustworthy they would have been fired from their tribe and kicked out to freeze in the cold and starve.

We can take power over ourselves, walk deliberately, in light and love in every way. There is no power if you don't respect yourself. If you are trusting untrustworthy people you are going to get hurt! Trust is not even something to expect from others, it is something for you to find in some people. Look for it, but don't expect it. You will only disappoint yourself.

I am always thrilled to meet someone genuinely trustworthy! It is rare! I always give thanks to Creator for that rare occurrence! And I value those people highly. They are few and far between today. And you attract trustworthy people by being trustworthy yourself.

We do tend to trust too freely, to trust the wrong people. But now that we have the knowledge about whom we can trust, we don't have to get burned by other people so much. We still respect them, we still respect their free will choice to be untrustworthy but we have our eyes open now. We have a torch with which to walk in our lives that helps us be safer and more peaceful. We have also learned where self-respect comes from, how to empower ourselves, and how to stand more fully in our power by being accountable and truthful and consistent and reliable and following through.

As we stand in our power we become more powerful healers. We are able to do more energetically in union with Creator. Becoming trustworthy is a spiritual practice for sure! Everyone should be working on some type of personal spiritual healing all the time. Becoming trustworthy is one of these personal spiritual healing practices. It would be good for all of us to be healed from any kind of victimhood. When you know you are trustworthy, then that is very good healing for yourself, but it takes daily practice.

Whom can you trust if you cannot trust yourself? Whom should you trust? Yourself! Implicitly! And you can heal the world by being trustworthy. What a breath of fresh air you become to the world! People will flock to you because they can trust you!

# References

Confucius, , Ames, R. T., & Rosemont, H. (1998). *The analects of Confucius: A philosophical translation.* New York: Ballantine Pub. Group.

Gulen, F., & Unal, A. (2004). *Key concepts in the practice of Sufism: Emerald hills of the heart.* Rutherford, N.J: Fountain

Ko͞, K., & Ṯhanissaro, . (2005). *Pure and simple: Teachings of a Thai Buddhist laywoman.* Boston: Wisdom Publications.

Miller, J. G. (1998). *Personal accountability: Powerful and practical ideas for you and your organization.* Brighton, Colo: Denver Press.

Nhât, H. (1999). *The heart of the Buddha's teaching: Transforming suffering into peace, joy & liberation : the four noble truths, the noble eightfold path, and other basic Buddhist teachings.* New York: Broadway Books.

Qushayrī, A. -K. H., Knysh, A. D., Eissa, M. S., & Centre for Muslim Contribution to Civilization. (2007). *Al-Qushayri's Epistle on Sufism: Al-Risala al-qushayriyya fi 'ilm al-tasawwuf.* Reading, UK: Garnet Pub.

Raefiel, A. (2002). *Getting to the heart: A journey of soul transformation and spiritual enlightenment.* Victoria, B.C: Trafford.

Rosen, K. (2008). *Time Management for Sales Professionals*

Rosen, K. (2004). *Complete idiot's guide to cold calling.* Indianapolis, IN: Alpha Book

Trungpa, C., & Baker, J. (1973). *Cutting through spiritual materialism.* Berkeley: Shambhala.

Wahls, M. (2011). *The Shaman speaks: How to use the power of Shamanism to heal your life now.* Ann Arbor, MI: Marvelous Spirit Press

## Web Resources

http://www.trans4mind.com

http://en.wikipedia.org/wiki/Accountability

http://www.orgcoach.net/newsletter/dec2004.html

http://www.mahatma.co.uk/p175.htm

http://www.universal-tao.com/article/something.html

http://www.circleofa.org/articles/GoodIntentions.php

http://www.coping.org/growth/trust.htm

http://www.shamanelder.com/impeccability.htm

www.employeedevelopmentsolutions.com/peoplefirst/v1n1personalaccountability.htm

www.allbusiness.com/sales/selling-techniques-strategic-selling/3910565-1.html

## About the Author

Shaman Elder Maggie Wahls has been practicing Shamanism since her grandmother, a traditional indigenous Shaman, began teaching her at age three. She has written and published many articles including a book titled The Shaman Speaks and teaches an online apprenticeship course in traditional Shamanism at www.shamanelder.com. She is available for a FREE consultation and will not turn anyone away.

Lightning Source UK Ltd.
Milton Keynes UK
UKOW062034090713

213518UK00010B/542/P